Chickens

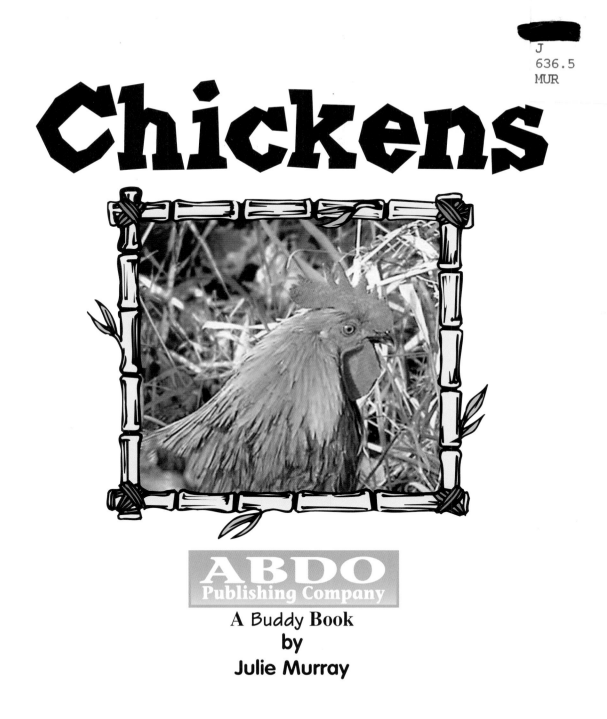

ABDO
Publishing Company

A Buddy Book
by
Julie Murray

VISIT US AT
www.abdopub.com

Published by Buddy Books, an imprint of ABDO Publishing Company, 4940 Viking Drive, Suite 622, Edina, Minnesota 55435. Copyright © 2002 by Abdo Consulting Group, Inc. International copyrights reserved in all countries. No part of this book may be reproduced in any form without written permission from the publisher.

Printed in the United States.

Edited by: Christy DeVillier
Contributing Editors: Matt Ray, Michael P. Goecke
Graphic Design: Maria Hosley
Image Research: Deborah Coldiron
Photographs: Photodisc

Library of Congress Cataloging-in-Publication Data

Murray, Julie, 1969-
  Chickens/Julie Murray.
      p. cm. — (Animal kingdom)
  Summary: An introduction to the physical characteristics, behavior, and different breeds of chickens.
  ISBN 1-57765-649-0
    1. Chickens—Juvenile literature. [1. Chickens.] I. Title. II. Animal kingdom
  (Edina, Minn.)

SF487.5 .M87 2002
636.5—dc21

                                        2001046371

Contents

Chickens

Chickens came from the jungles of Asia. People tamed chickens over 5,000 years ago. Today most chickens live on farms across the world. But some chickens still live in the wild.

Chickens live all over the world.

Sometimes, we call chickens poultry. Poultry can be ducks, turkey, and geese, too. Birds that people raise for food are poultry. Poultry farmers sell eggs and meat.

Hens And Roosters

We call female chickens hens. They make a "cluck, cluck" sound.

We call male chickens roosters. Roosters are bigger than hens. They crow "cock-a-doodle-doo" at sunrise every morning.

comb

wattle

Both hens and roosters have combs and wattles. A chicken's red comb stands up on its head. A chicken's red wattle hangs below its beak. A rooster's comb and wattle are bigger than a hen's.

What They Are Like

Chickens spend their day pecking and scratching. Chickens clean themselves many times a day, too. Preening keeps their feathers clean. A chicken preens by running its beak through its feathers. Chickens also take dust baths to stay clean. Dust baths get rid of insects on chickens.

Have you ever called someone a chicken? Was it because they were scared of something? Chickens get scared easily. They move their wings back and forth when they are afraid.

Breeds of Chickens

There are more than 60 chicken breeds. Each breed is a different kind of chicken. One breed lays a lot of eggs. Another breed gives a lot of meat. Some people breed chickens to win prizes at shows. These are show chickens.

Do you ever eat eggs for breakfast? Did these eggs come from a white shell? If so, you probably had eggs from a leghorn chicken. The leghorn chicken lays white eggs. Stores across America sell leghorn chicken eggs.

The Pecking Order

Chickens like to be together in flocks. Every flock of chickens has a **pecking order**. The first chicken in the pecking order is the leader. The leader is the boss of the other chickens. The leader pecks other chickens so they know who is boss.

All chickens know their place in the flock's pecking order. Each chicken bosses the chickens below it. The last chicken in the pecking order has no one to boss.

Chicken flocks follow a pecking order.

Where They Live

Most chickens live on factory farms. Factory farms can be very big. Some farms have more than 100,000 chickens in one building. These chickens live inside small cages.

Some farmers raise free-range chickens on small farms. Free-range chickens have more space to run around. They spend the night in a hen house or a chicken coop. A chicken coop keeps chickens safe from raccoons and foxes.

Some chickens live on small farms like this one.

What
They Eat

Free-range chickens eat insects like crickets and grasshoppers. Farmers feed chickens corn and scratch. Scratch is a special mix of grains. Chickens also eat lettuce, grapes, cooked spaghetti, sunflower seeds, and bread.

Chickens eat small stones along with their food.

Chickens do not chew their food. Chickens break up food in their gizzards. The gizzard needs tiny stones to break up the chicken's food. So, chickens eat small stones off the ground. Some farmers give chickens grit to eat. Grit is made of small, broken stones.

Chicks

Baby chickens are chicks. Chicks make a "peep-peep" sound. Chicks stay inside their eggs for about three weeks. The mother hen sits on her eggs until they hatch. We call this brooding.

Chicks hatch from eggs.

19

Chicks are cold and tired after pecking out of their eggs. The mother hen keeps her chicks warm. Chicks follow the hen and learn how to peck. In 20 weeks, female chicks grow into adult hens. At this time, they can begin laying their own eggs.

A mother hen keeps an eye on her chicks.

Important Words

brood to sit on eggs to hatch them.

comb the reddish skin standing up on a chicken's head.

gizzard the body part of a bird that breaks up food.

grit small, broken rocks that a farmer gives a chicken to eat.

pecking order order of leaders in a chicken flock.

poultry birds that farmers raise for food.

preening what birds do to clean their feathers.

wattle the flap of skin that hangs from a chicken's throat.

Web Sites

Chickens

www.kidsfarm.com
Hear chicks peep and see pictures of hens, roosters, and chicks.

Poultry Breeds

www.ansi.okstate.edu/poultry/
This web site features information on many kinds of chickens.

The Other Side of the Chicken

homestead.juno.com/cuttle/files/chick.html
The author of this web site keeps chickens as pets.

Index